creepy creatures

CONTENTS

Published by Creative Education
P.O. Box 227, Mankato, Minnesota 56002
Creative Education is an imprint of
The Creative Company
www.thecreativecompany.us

Design and production by Ellen Huber
Art direction by Rita Marshall
Printed by Corporate Graphics
in the United States of America

Photographs by 123RF (Adrian Hillman, Vukasin Ilic,
Pavel Konovalov, Dmitry Margolin), Getty Images (Tim
Laman, Medford Taylor), iStockphoto (Noam Armonn,
Evgeniy Ayupov, Eric Isselée, Cathy Keifer), National
Geographic Image Collection (Mark Moffett/Minden
Pictures), Shutterstock (Evgeniy Ayupov, Steve Byland,
Gaga, Alexander Kolomietz, Jens Stolt)

Library of Congress Cataloging-in-Publication Data
Bodden, Valerie.
Mantises / by Valerie Bodden.
p. cm. — (Creepy creatures)
Summary: A basic introduction to mantises, examining
where they live, how they grow, what they eat, and
the unique traits that help to define them, such as
their ability to rotate their heads.
Includes index.
ISBN 978-1-58341-994-6
1. Mantodea—Juvenile literature. I. Title. II. Series.
QL505.83.B63 2011
595.7'27—dc22   2009052520
CPSIA: 040110 PO1135

First Edition
9 8 7 6 5 4 3 2 1

mantises

VALERIE BODDEN

CREATIVE **C** EDUCATION

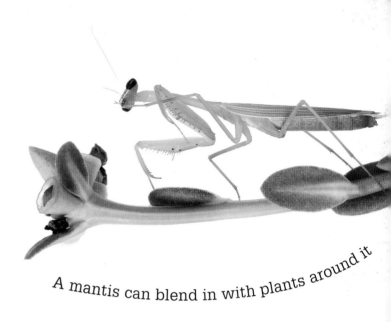

A mantis can blend in with plants around it

You are walking through a field of tall grass. Suddenly you spot a strange shape on a weed. It is a long, thin bug with bent front legs. It is a mantis!

Mantises are also called praying mantises or mantids. They are **insects**. A mantis's body has three main parts. Its head looks like a triangle. Mantises have big eyes and two **antennae** (*an-TEH-nee*). They have six legs. Most mantises have wings, too.

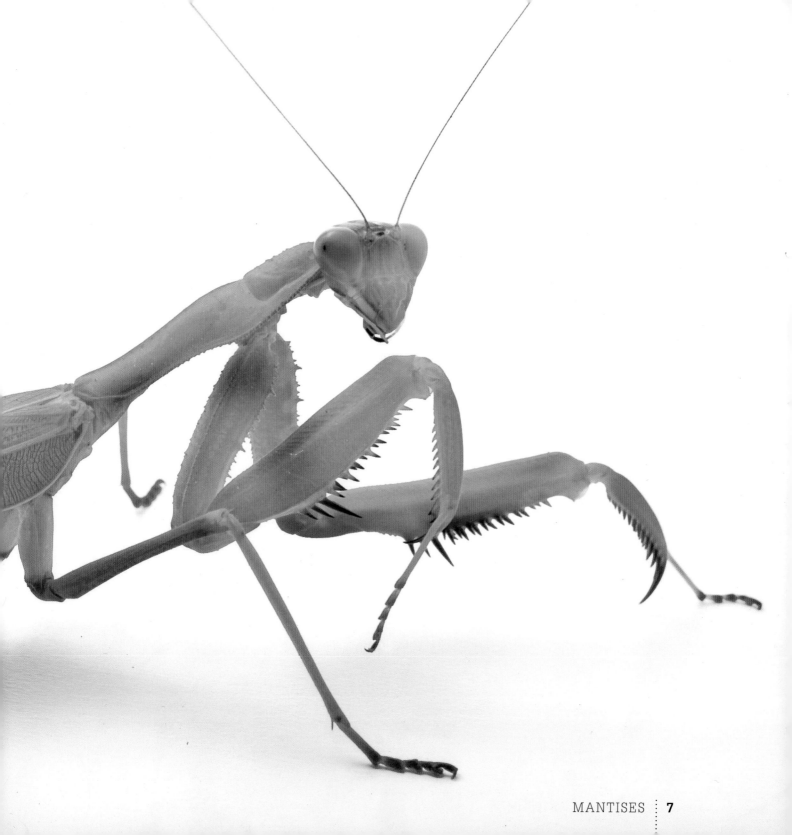

Some mantises are about as long as your finger. But others can be almost as long as a ruler! Mantises are usually green or brown. But some are pink or white.

Mantises can be many colors and sizes

There are about 2,000 different kinds of mantises. The Carolina mantis can be found in southern parts of the United States. Twig mantises are brown and bumpy. They look like sticks.

The ghost mantis lives in Africa and looks like a leaf

A mantis spreads its wings to fly away from predators

Mantises live in warm places. They can live in rainforests, deserts, and grasslands. Mantises have to watch out for **predators**. Monkeys, bats, and birds all eat mantises.

After a mantis molts for the last time, it becomes an adult

Mother mantises lay hundreds of eggs. Baby mantises are called nymphs (*NIMFS*). Nymphs look like small adult mantises. But they do not have wings. As they grow, the nymphs get too big for their skin. They **molt** so they can keep growing. The nymphs grow wings, too. Mantises usually live less than a year.

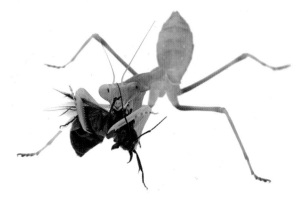

Most mantises eat insects and spiders. Some big mantises can eat frogs! Mantises sit still and wait for **prey** to come near. Then they grab the prey with their front legs and eat it.

A mantis catches and eats its prey very quickly

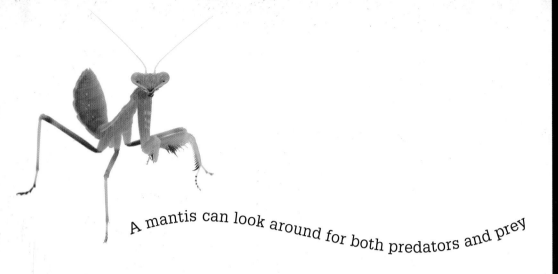

A mantis can look around for both predators and prey

Mantises are good hunters because they can see well with their big eyes. They can also turn their heads from side to side. Mantises are the only insects that can do this.

People in Africa used to think mantises were **gods**. In France, people thought mantises could show lost kids the way home. It can be fun finding and watching these big-eyed creepy creatures!

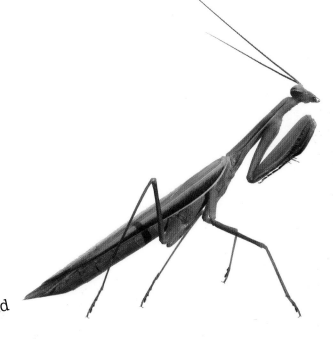

Mantises are found in countries all around the world

MAKE A MANTIS

You can make your own mantis with some colored paper and pipe cleaners! First, cut a large triangle out of a piece of stiff colored paper. Then cut two small circles out of different-colored paper. Glue them to the triangle for eyes. Glue two pipe cleaners to the top of the triangle for antennae. Glue a Popsicle stick to the bottom of the triangle. Have fun with your mantis puppet!

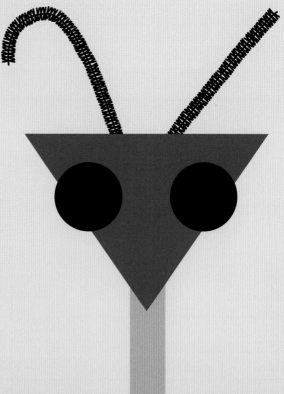

GLOSSARY

antennae: feelers on the heads of some bugs that are used to touch, smell, and taste things

gods: beings that people think have special powers and control the world

insects: small animals with three body parts and six legs; most have two pairs of wings, too

molt: to lose a shell or layer of skin and grow a new, larger one

predators: animals that kill and eat other animals

prey: animals that are killed and eaten by other animals

READ MORE

Goldish, Meish. *Deadly Praying Mantises*. New York: Bearport Publishing, 2008.

Sexton, Colleen. *Praying Mantises*. Minneapolis: Bellwether Media, 2007.

WEB SITES

Enchanted Learning: Praying Mantid
http://www.enchantedlearning.com/subjects/insects/mantids/Prayingmantidprintout.shtml
Learn more about mantises and print a mantis picture to color.

National Geographic Kids Creature Feature: Praying Mantids
http://kids.nationalgeographic.com/Animals/CreatureFeature/Praying-mantid
Check out pictures and videos of mantises.

INDEX